PURPOSELY DRIVEN POEMS

How to Empower Your Faith,
Hope and
Love for All Ages

BE INSPIRED

INSPIRE OTHERS

Bill Rockefeller

The Rockefeller Collection
Volume I

Battle Press
SATELLITE BEACH, FLORIDA

PURPOSELY DRIVEN POEMS
How to Empower Your Faith, Hope, and Love for All Ages

Be Inspired
Inspire Others

The Rockefeller Collection, Volume I

Copyright © 2021 by Bill Rockefeller.

All rights reserved. No part of this book may be used or reproduced by any means, graphic, electronic or mechanical, including photocopying, recording, taping or by any information storage retrieval system without the written permission of the author or publisher except in the case of brief quotations embodied in critical articles and reviews.

Books may be ordered through booksellers or by visiting:

purposelydrivenpoems@gmail.com
Purposelydrivenpoems.com

Or

Battle Press
steve@battlepress.media
www.battlepress.media

ISBN: 978-1-7374-9915-2 (SC)
ISBN: 978-1-7374-9916-9 (HC)
ISBN: 979-8-9862-6322-9 (eBook)

Library of Congress Control Number: 2022903358

First Edition

PURPOSELY DRIVEN POEMS

To get your **FREE** copy of Bill Rockefeller's *The Ten Commandments In Poetry*, click on the link below:

Fill out the form with your name and email address, and in the 'Message' section indicate:

- Title of book: **The Ten Commandments In Poetry**
- Whether you want a **PDF** or **EPUB** file.

Free Book Link:
https://battlepress.media/?page_id=13

Your book will be emailed to you ENJOY!

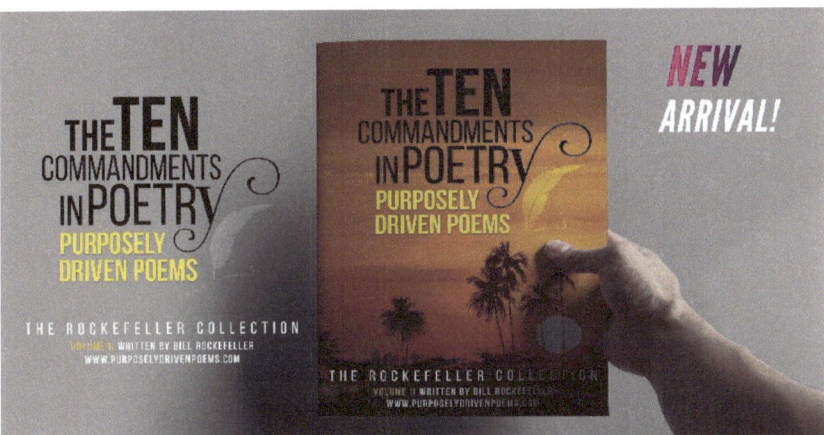

*If you enjoy **Purposely Driven Poems**, I would really appreciate a short review, your help in spreading the word is highly valued and reviews make it much easier for readers to find the book.*

Review Link:
https://www.amazon.com/review/create-review/?ie=UTF8&channel=glance-detail&asin=B0B324N77R

ACKNOWLEDGEMENTS

I'd like to acknowledge and recommend some material that helped me become inspired with ideas that grew into the poetry and antidotes of this book. The 1st is Rick Warren and *The Purpose Driven Life* which inspired more than poems and more than thoughts but spiritual intentions I would have never thought of.

Man's Search For Meaning by Victor Frankel was another book that resonates in my mind. The forward of that book was by Harold Kushner, who said that if a book has 1 passage, 1 idea with the power to change a person's life that alone justifies reading it, re reading it and finding room for it on one's shelf. He has authored some of the best sellers like, *Living A Life That Matters* and *When All You Ever Wanted Is Not Enough*, these enlightening books gave me an insight with the spiritual realization that supported my rebirth accepting Jesus Christ as my saviour.

Then the Holy Spirit sparked me a purpose, that not only helped myself be reminded, but I hope it helps others. Along with the entertaining and enlightening poems matched by a scripture from the Bible gave more of an impact to the poem and personal awareness of walking in, the Fruits of the spirit.

To call this into your universe can perpetuate a growth of awareness and a higher calling to you. With the influences of the scriptures and its teachings we all can claim better daily actions to come.

TABLE OF CONTENTS

ACKNOWLEDGEMENTS 4	FRIENDS OR FOE 37
TABLE OF CONTENTS 5	YOUR LIGHT 38
INTRODUCTION 7	MEANT TO BE 39
BELIEVE 8	THE HAND OF GOD 40
THANKS 9	EVER FIND 41
THE BIBLE STORY 10	SO WILL YOU 42
A LITTLE HUG 11	IN STYLE 43
A LOVE 12	WHILE IT CAN 44
THE PEN 13	TRY 45
FAITH 14	THE SAME 46
HOPE 15	SOULMATE 47
HOPE AND FAITH 16	NOW 48
EACH PURPOSE 17	I HOPE YOU UNDERSTAND ... 49
THE HORSE THAT YOU RIDE 18	ONE BY ONE 50
THE STEPS 19	SHOUT 51
A SEED 20	THE GIFT 52
SMART I PHONE 21	ALL YOU GOT 53
POCKET OF FAITH 22	THIS RESIDENCE 54
COLOR OF HOPE 23	THE LORDS GRAPES 55
LOVE FLOWS FREE 24	HIS CROWN 56
SIT BACK AND SMILE 25	JUST PRAY 57
DO SOMETHING 26	FAMILY TREE 58
WINNING WALK 27	OUR PURPOSE 59
COUNTING ON YOU 28	BEAUTIFUL SMILE 60
HAVING FUN 29	BLESSINGS 61
YOUR DESTINY 30	LISTEN SOME MORE 62
MY CLOSEST FRIEND 31	MEANT TO BE 63
ANOTHER YOU 32	SALVATION 64
LORDS ARMOUR 33	THE PREACHER MAN 65
OK 34	KEEP US STRONG 66
LIFE IS TOO SHORT 35	EVERY TIME 67
SPIRIT OF LIFE 36	SHAPED FOR SERVING GOD 68

OUR CHALLENGE… 69	CULTIVATE YOUR DREAMS 102
HIDDEN SO WELL 70	NEVER FORGOT 103
WHEN YOU TRY 71	JESUS TELLS US SO 104
GIFT OF INSIGHT 72	EVER SO STRONG 105
NO MISTAKES 73	BE 106
YOUR PURPOSE 74	STILL 107
AMEN 75	OURS TO HOLD 108
TO OBTAIN FAITH 76	ECHO TODAY 109
ME AND YOU 77	THE MESSAGE 110
SHINING ON YOU 78	I AM CONTENT 111
STAND TALL 79	TO FLOW 112
EVERYTHING 80	DISGUISE 113
WORDS 81	ON FIRE 114
LORD GODS POEM 82	VICTORY 115
FAITH IS A SONG 83	ANOTHER BEAUTIFUL DAY 116
SO GOOD 84	THE MIGHT 117
YOU ARE NEVER ALONE 85	SHINE 118
BEFORE 86	HOPE TODAY 119
BRIGHTEN YOUR DAY 87	A GOOD TIME 120
THE TONGUE 88	ALLOW IT TO BE 121
GOOD OLD TIME 89	ALL IT CAN BE 122
CHRISTMAS DAY 90	GRATITUDE 123
START 91	MY DESTINY 124
TREE OF FAITH 92	PURPOSELY DRIVEN 125
GOD'S DRONES 93	
THE SONG OF LIFE 94	
EACH STEP 95	
OUR LORD 96	
A SPIRIT 97	
ONE DAY 98	
EVERYBODY 99	
EVERY HOUR 100	
CAN'T BE DENIED 101	

INTRODUCTION

The first poem was called BELIEVE. It was admired by people who encouraged me to continue. The next day GOD woke me at dawn to start writing. My workmanship for the lord was started. Three to four a day came out on paper written in pencil. Sparked by my Holy Spirit I have written hundreds. Later on, I found a way to speak them into my phone on beautiful landscapes. Asking of Google, I received many matching scriptures, and I started learning, some I never heard of before. Therefore, I was able to find the most appropriate, to compliment the message in the poem.

I believe the Lord was preparing me with seeds of wisdom by word. Which only fueled my Poems with passion. My purpose had started, and so I recognized it. This insight ignited the fruits of my Spirit, which I was able to capture on paper. Poems and Scriptures. A higher thought level, calling to my life. Here are 118 Poems and Scriptures Volume 1. They can be read and re-read or as Mr. Franklin said, put on your shelf. They can be mounted on Canvass for any wall. Furthermore, it enabled me to learn scriptures and navigate through "The Bible" building a better understanding and knowledge of word and deed. A purpose for myself and my poetry. It developed into a workmanship for the lord. In Greek workmanship means poem. Each one complimented by a Bible scripture. I truly, hope all readers, get their self-rewarding chance to empower their faith, hope and love, while sharing the fruits of their spirit, as Ambassadors to Christ Jesus. A new ambassador to the Lord is born every second. **AMEN**

"Our life is a daily journey let's make sure we are headed in the right direction."

Bill Rockefeller

PURPOSELYDRIVENPOEMS.COM

BELIEVE

We follow the roads
to take us through States
we captain the vessel
that carries our faith
Directions we choose
can happen at will
with trials and changes
we have to fulfil
but as crazy
as it all seems to be
it's incisive design
can change like a dream
the purpose of life
confusing at times
a supernatural gift some of us find
so mighty and amazing, so much to achieve
one thing is certain
you have to believe

MARK 11:24
*Therefore, I say to you
whatsoever you desire, when we pray
believe you receive them, and you shall have
them.*

THANKS

We all need togetherness
we all need love
we all need hope
so we pray to above
as we wait and we wonder
about the times to come
with all the blessings
that are already around us
can we count them one by one
yes it seems to be
so easy to add up all the
money in your bank
but have you counted
all your blessings
and given God your thanks

2nd CORINTHIANS 2:14
Now thanks be unto God, which always causeth us to triumph in Christ, and maketh manifest the saviour of his knowledge by us in every place.

PURPOSELY DRIVEN POEMS

THE BIBLE STORY

The Bible contains the mind of God the state of man
the way of salvation the doom of the sinners
and happiness of believers. Its doctrines are holy,
its stories are binding, its histories are true
and it's decisions are immutable.

Read it to be wise, believe it to be safe and protected.
To be holy it contains the light to direct you,
food to support you, and comfort to cheer you.
Here Paradise is restored, Heaven opens,
the gates of hell are disclosed and

Christ is the grand subject of the glory of God.
It should fill the mind, meaning of
the hearts and guide the feet.
Read it slowly, frequently and prayerfully.

It holds a chest of gems and knowledge with glory,
pleasure and life. It introduces the higher of
responsibilities and will condemn all who
trifle with its secret contents.

It's been translated into 1,100 languages,
placed in 190 countries and reached
distributions of 1.8 billion.

PURPOSELYDRIVENPOEMS.COM

A LITTLE HUG

I was born on this planet without a care
God knew as I grew
I would have a lot to share
to all who read these poems of life
I hope they bring you a smile and delight
I wrote these poems for the fortunate few
who read with feeling just like you
yet since my time will soon be gone
I hope you enjoy them, and they carry on
not knowing when our spirits might meet
if you can't send me an email or a tweet
if you arrive in heaven up above
Just give my spirit
a little hug

PSALMS 18:23
*Though he had commanded the clouds from up above,
and open the doors to heaven.*

A LOVE

A Love is fast
A Love is slow
Love is everywhere that we go
A Love is strong
A Love is weak
Love is everything that we seek
A Love can't run
A Love can't hide
but Love can live
and Love can thrive
A Love is words
A love is songs
and in your heart
Love always belongs

JOHN 15:12
This is my commandment that you shall love one another as I have loved you.

THE PEN

I give life to these words
with a pen right here
for people to read any day of the year
they pass out feelings
I cannot deny
some have a smile on their face
or a tear in their eye
I write these words
neither wrong nor right
just penned on paper
to share with delight
words explain life
all writers may try
but without a pen
these words would die

JERIMIAH 17
The sin of Judah is written with a pen
of iron and with the point of a diamond
It is graven upon the tablet
of their heart and upon
the horns of your altars.

FAITH

Faith has no color
Faith has no size
Faith has no shape
you can see
with your eyes
Faith is always significant
with a spiritual sound
and like the air that we breathe
thank God it's around

Hebrews 11:1
Faith is the substance of things hoped for
with the evidence not yet seen.

HOPE

Hope is a word
so small and so fine
Hope is the word
to inspire your mind
Hope is the feeling
that helps you to grow
very easy to take around
anywhere you go

ROMANS 15:13
Now the God of hope shall fill you with all the joy and peace in believing that ye may abound in hope through the power of the Holy Ghost.

HOPE AND FAITH

Hope is the fresh breath
we have come to recieve
to smooth out our
doubts that come in between
easy to grow
in all human beings
we call on our hope
by our heart held voice
prosperity speaks
for it is your choice
we only have moments
to choose how we act
with faith as our guide
we never look back
dreaming and deciding about things
we would like to do
when your faith makes the choice
you always shine through
it is definitely here
just to help you

JERIMIAH 17:7
Blessed is the man who trusts in the Lord,
And whose hope is the Lord.

PURPOSELYDRIVENPOEMS.COM

EACH PURPOSE

Each step that we take
leads us alluring in life
to seek out a mindset
proactively right
with directions of grandeur
reactions do flow
as time pushes us on
we stay on the go
enjoying what we have
with the pleasure we know
as our life
keeps moving forward
we are born to grow
so we welcome each purpose
God has to show

EPHESIANS 5:15
*See then that you walk circumspectly
not as fools, but as wise.*

PURPOSELY DRIVEN POEMS

THE HORSE THAT YOU RIDE

The power of purpose
is all that you need
to conquer the world so hard to believe
surrounded by anger - scolded by hate
laughed at with malice - accidents of fate
picked up with kindness
delivered by love
look up to the heavens
for the hope we thought of
there are but few situations in life
where only true vision
can help you see right
we all have our white horse
since deep down inside
while you are still able
to walk with your pride
make it so known with your stride
that the power of purpose
is the horse that you ride

ISAIAH 30:16
*But ye said no, we will flee upon horses
therefore shall ye flee, and we will ride upon
the swift
Therefore, shall they who pursue you
be swift?*

PURPOSELYDRIVENPOEMS.COM

THE STEPS

Each step in your life
creates readiness
Not to be harder, but to be in control
to establish an order in your daily life
your control is essential
in preparation for your purpose
and to reach your destiny
once you set your priorities in order
you awake each day determined and
eager with the principles
to pursue your purpose
don't worry about how many steps
or how far your journey is
be happy with how far
you have already come
just to realize this is one
crucial needed step

PSALMS 119:117
*Holding up that I may be safe and have regard
For your statutes continually my Lord,
Keep steady my steps.*

PURPOSELYDRIVENPOEMS.COM

PURPOSELY DRIVEN POEMS

A SEED

A seed of Faith
can grow in you
to bring you the strength
you never knew
it takes the word
and a little time
to come along
to polish your shine
a seed of faith
is all you need
followed by the word believe
use your patience
to seek and find
so your faith will grow
in your heart and mind

MATHEW 17:20
*If you have Faith as small as a mustard seed
nothing will be impossible for you.*

PURPOSELYDRIVENPOEMS.COM

SMART I PHONE

God has your number
You're never alone
He could reach you through
your Smart IPhone
He knows you're every call
He has your back if you should fall
He respects your honour and
circumstance
always giving you another chance
so wear his Armour - wear it proud
then you won't be taken down
keep your faith - let it be known
God has your back
You're never alone
He could reach you
through your Smart IPhone

PSALM I
Blessed Is the man that walketh not under the counsel of the ungodly, nor standeth in the way of sinners, Nor sitteth in the seat of the scornful.

PURPOSELYDRIVENPOEMS.COM

PURPOSELY DRIVEN POEMS

POCKET OF FAITH

A pocket of Faith is all you need
to sow the truth or plant the seed
A pocket of faith should always be in
your hand
so you are never lost
in neverland
a pocket of faith can be shared by you
with others who need a little faith too
A pocket of faith is easy to show
as you carefully cultivate
your spirit to grow
a pocket of Faith
can provide you the most
spiritual reach to your holy ghost
a pocket of faith means you believe
and so no your guardian angel
will never leave

ROMANS 10:17
*So then faith cometh by hearing
And hearing by the word of God.*

PURPOSELYDRIVENPOEMS.COM

COLOR OF HOPE

The color of hope
is whatever you use
it's your design to be
how you choose
the color of hope
blinding bright like the sun
It can flow forth with your actions
to inspire everyone
It's always defining
your individual soul
with the insight and promise
we all need to hold
It matches a style
that blends into your worth
every day that you wear it
and walk on this earth

ROMANS 12:12
*Rejoicing hope patient in tribulation
continuing instant in prayer.*

LOVE FLOWS FREE

The grace of giving
starts with God
for all we have he brings upon
he comes in times
we need him most
with timing so right
for he is our host
with an open heart
we understand the facts
and the life
we carry on our backs
to engage our moments
that adorn us older
younger years
were a time more bolder
if we give our most
in times we can
see a turning point
in the heart of man
it is a place in each
where our love flows free
yes, that's the way
God wanted it to be

ROMANS 13:8
*Owe no one anything,
except to love each other for the one
who loves another has fulfilled the law.*

PURPOSELYDRIVENPOEMS.COM

PURPOSELY DRIVEN POEMS

SIT BACK AND SMILE

It's a great life
that's how we live
we expect all we need
so we move on
every day with our mind
shifting memories of the past
most magnificent times
we do what we need
for happiness to live
as we pass out some love
it is easy to give
just do It with style
then at the end of each day
you can sit back and smile

ROMANS 12:2
*And be not conformed to this world:
but be ye transformed by the renewing of your mind,
that ye may prove what is that good,
and acceptable, and perfect, will of God.*

PURPOSELYDRIVENPOEMS.COM

PURPOSELY DRIVEN POEMS

DO SOMETHING

We could never add
quality to our life
by worrying
we could never
change the future by fear
It never gave us
any extra quality time
in our life
to do what our sound mind
has to do here
with our living moments
in the days that amount to years
with freedom to do anything
with the time you have
right here
do something
have no fear

2ND TIMOTHY 1:7
*For God Hath not given us the spirit of fear,
but of power, and of love and a sound mind.*

PURPOSELYDRIVENPOEMS.COM

WINNING WALK

In the beginning we could only crawl
then we learned to stand
and walk real tall
but soon we learned the charm of speech
for truth or lies to be in our reach
something we can never stop
like the moves we make
to put us on top
your style is easy as you slide on through
proactive abundant and progressive too
sometimes so easy some days are hard
some times are bright when your light is on
you have learned
to do more than to think and talk
so lead your life
with the winning walk

1 JOHN 4:4
You are from God, little children, and have overcome them; because greater is He, who is in you than he who is in the world.

COUNTING ON YOU

Spiritual growth
starts in your mind
it reaches your heart
a piece at a time
creating a path
for others to find
we all walk in unison
so our spirit can shine
in many directions
in our moments of time
they pull us each day
while the Bible shares the lessons
so we don't go astray
as you help
your spirit to grow
with the wisdom to get through
you may help
someone else
whose spirit is counting on you

LUKE 2:40
*And the child grew
and waxed strong in spirit, filled with wisdom
and the grace of God was upon him.*

PURPOSELYDRIVENPOEMS.COM

HAVING FUN

Count your blessings
one by one
start with a morning
and a rising Sun
thank God for the air
so that you breathe
and move around the world
with the greatest of ease
we learn to count
when we are very young
so keep counting your blessings
while you're having fun

PSALMS 103:2
*Bless the Lord all my soul
and let's not forget all his benefits.*

PURPOSELY DRIVEN POEMS

YOUR DESTINY

We all have a purpose
we all have a style
everyday so encircling
allowing us to smile
the ardor of our life
the moves that we make
bring us to a place
where our memories find today
so much of our talent
takes us through each day
without its use
it will disintegrate away
to know what this means
is vital to your heart
holding your priorities
not to break apart
nothing can separate
what your vision can see
while God is the conductor
of your destiny

JEREMIAH 29:11
For I know the plans that I had for you
the Lord declared.
Plans for abundance and calamity.
To give you a future and a hope.

PURPOSELYDRIVENPOEMS.COM

MY CLOSEST FRIEND

Feed your body
feed your mind
feed your spirit all the time
your body is your temple
you should know
you must do your best
to help it grow
it needs you and you need it
you are born together
for the perfect fit
always with you close
to provide your illuminating shine
you depend on it
all the time
always remember right till the end
your Spirit is your closest friend

2 TIMOTHY 1:7
For God has not given us a spirit of fear,
but of power and love and a sound mind.

PURPOSELYDRIVENPOEMS.COM

PURPOSELY DRIVEN POEMS

ANOTHER YOU

The words that come
from your open mouth
can be a whisper or a shout
they can lift your spirit
or save your soul
fix any broken pieces
to keep you whole
let the days that come
with so much to do
satisfy the deepest desires
you find true
with all those special things
that only you can do
because there will never be
another you

MATTHEW 7:21
*Not everyone that says unto me, Lord
Shall enter the gates of heaven,
But he that doeth the will of my father,
who is in heaven.*

PURPOSELYDRIVENPOEMS.COM

PURPOSELY DRIVEN POEMS

LORDS ARMOUR

His love comes
with no condition
His love comes
because it can
Yet he expects
no gifts or presents
only to listen
to his ten commands
it sounds pretty simple
and easy to do
whenever temptation
entices your spirit
you must never
let it through
I wear the lord's armour
to protect me
how about you?

EPHESIANS 6:11
*Put on the whole armour of God
that ye may be able to stand against
the wiles of the Devil.*

PURPOSELYDRIVENPOEMS.COM

OK

We breed on the Earth
never getting much younger
the critics of life bring you over or under
I proceed each day with my normal sway
exceptionally tuned
to go on my way
but words only heard
come on spewing out
lightning and thunder
plummets in my way
just to bring me down under
I must understand
the way to convey
the fruits of the spirit
to stay with me all day
continuing to have a brighter say
Lord, My Lord make it OK

ROMANS 8:1
*Therefore, now no condemnation
To those that live with Christ Jesus,
to those who walk not after the flesh
but after the spirit.*

PURPOSELYDRIVENPOEMS.COM

PURPOSELY DRIVEN POEMS

LIFE IS TOO SHORT

Life is too short
to waste a minute
and since you are here
you're already right in it
make it the best
that you carefully can
every day is yours
at your command
allow no one to exchange
or persuade to
take away your sway
nor the kaleidoscope
you view on a sunny day

PSALMS 119:117
*Holding up that I may be safe and have regard
for your statutes continually my Lord,
keep steady my steps.*

PURPOSELY DRIVEN POEMS

SPIRIT OF LIFE

The spirit of life
lives in us all
the more we believe
the less we will fall
and the greater that we will hear
His tune when he calls
God helps us with directions
that are easy to follow
so we can grow up
not to be spiritually shallow
our Faith provides
dynamic confidence
so everywhere we go
our spirit of life
is the star of the show

JOHN 6:63
*It is the spirit who gives
life, the flesh provides nothing.
The words I speak unto you
they are spirit and they are life.*

PURPOSELYDRIVENPOEMS.COM

FRIENDS OR FOE

Thank you, Jesus,
you did me right
you allow my feet
to walk under your light
what was once
detrimentally dark
is now brilliant and bright
I follow your words
which teach me right
these times and scriptures
I have come to know
keep whispering to me
that is how I grow
I shall pass them forward
wherever I go
the words I can share
with friends or foe

PSALM 37:4
*Delight thyself also in the Lord
and he will give you the desires of your heart.*

PURPOSELY DRIVEN POEMS

YOUR LIGHT

Refuse to be a victim
stand for your rights
you are not to be a victim
don't lose the fight
refuse to be victimized
use the power in your life
his breath gave you a spirit
and your Faith gives you the might
victory starts in thinking
turn on your light
the thoughts you hold inside
may help you shine so bright
let them out let them be
turn on your light

PSALM 119:73
You made me, you created me.
Now give me the sense to follow you.

PURPOSELYDRIVENPOEMS.COM

PURPOSELY DRIVEN POEMS

MEANT TO BE

With my spare moments of thought
and my amusing situations of time
with my moments in motion
ideas come to mind
today is my day
but how I got here
each cloud
rains down the memories
of all my past years
so I think
as far back as I can see
today I am still alive
I guess
it was meant to be

PSALMS 40:8
I delight to do thy will, O my God:
yea, thy law is within my heart.

THE HAND OF GOD

We all believe in something
or we wouldn't be here
we all fortify the purpose
that we hold dear
as he guides our steps
our road becomes clear
good decisions are made
when your Holy Spirit can hear
It is never too easy
but it never is that hard
when your heart is led
by the hand of God

1 PETER 5:6
*Humble yourself therefore
under the mighty hand of God.
That he may exalt you in due time.*

EVER FIND

Thank you Jesus
You did me right
You allow my feet
to walk under your light
the days of dark are now so bright
as I follow your words
which teach me right
these times and your scriptures
have been talking to me
they help me now
to be able to see
you set the example Jesus
how to be refined
to live the best life
we could ever find

JUDE 1:21
Keep yourself in the love of God,
Looking for the mercy of our lord
Jesus Christ unto eternal life.

SO WILL YOU

Faith is the substance of things
Hoped for with the evidence
not yet seen
able to grow in all human beings
we call on our faith
as our weapon of choice
created in our hearts
delivered by our inner voice
we only have moments
to choose how we act
with faith as our guide
we will never look back
to be dreaming about things
we plan to do
when your faith stands tall
so will you

HEBREWS 11:1
*Faith is the substance of things
hoped for with the evidence not yet seen.*

IN STYLE

One day at a time
we don't need more
what we're doing today
we never done before
just give it your best
give it a smile
keep walking in Faith
it's always in style

2ND CORINTHIANS 5:7
For we walk by faith not by sight.

WHILE IT CAN

We are like the trees
we grow up on the land
calling forth fruit
spirits understand
each fruit from the tree
can be measured with a sense of taste
what is right and useful
and it doesn't grow to waste
a good man's treasures
brings forth his prize
the evil man's treasure
is never too wise
You are the tree
wherever you stand
let your fruit of the spirit
flow while it can

GALATIANS 5:22
But the fruit of the spirit is love, joy, peace, long suffering, gentleness, goodness, and faith.

PURPOSELY DRIVEN POEMS

TRY

Which part of my heart
what space in my soul
keeps me together
with the way I have grown
we all have a reason
to want a piece of the pie
we all have the ability
not to give up
but try

LAMENTATIONS 3:40
*Let us search and try our ways
and turn again to the Lord.*

PURPOSELYDRIVENPOEMS.COM

PURPOSELY DRIVEN POEMS

THE SAME

Each day has a sunset
unique as its own
If we're lucky to catch it
then it is a beauty
to be known
visions of light
to start the new day
like a spark or a fire
from the family of flames
each day explodes
in unknown fame
to end as it does
but they all
start the same

JAMES 12:3
Count it all joy when you fall into diverse temptations, knowing this that the trying of your faith worketh patience.

PURPOSELYDRIVENPOEMS.COM

PURPOSELY DRIVEN POEMS

SOULMATE

You are one of a kind
as you walk on by
more than a look
catches my eye
with a melody of communication
we stand the chance
of tenderness and friendship
a slow whisper of romance
or the sound of live music
that starts you to prance
which can grow into promenades
that add years
to your dance
with a touch yet to feel and see
our beauty together
in harmony
together two people
sharing a casual fate
just might have each
found a true soulmate

GENESIS 2:22
*The Lord God fashioned into a woman
the rib, He had taken from the man.
and brought her to the man.*

PURPOSELYDRIVENPOEMS.COM

PURPOSELY DRIVEN POEMS

NOW

I'm here for a moment
a moment in time
day-by-day
each moment is mine
sometimes a mystery is all I can see
but day-by-day things come to be
I danced on many glorious stages
turned many full pages
slipped through many crammed crowds
but each moment I'm living
is my moment of now

PSALMS 37:24
*Be of good courage
and he shall strengthen your heart
all ye that hope in the Lord.*

I HOPE YOU UNDERSTAND

I stand for the flag
I kneel for the cross
each day is my delight
I have no loss
multiplying my efforts
like the man on the cross
sacred so simple
a genuine design
Jesus speaks wisdom
his words flash in my mind
be thankful be helpful
and pray when you can
Blessings will follow
I hope you understand

1 CORINTHIANS 15:57
*But thanks be to God
which give us the victory
through our lord Jesus Christ.*

PURPOSELY DRIVEN POEMS

ONE BY ONE

Wherever you are
wherever you go
God's grace is all around you
through rain, sleet, or snow
during sunny days or
in trying times
His words of promise come through
to deliver a covenant that binds
he does it all since the beginning of time
Jew, Gentile no matter his mind
Our Father in Heaven gave us his son
to lay down his life
for forgiveness to come
he still teaches us all
for his work is not done
that is why
we share his scriptures together
one by one

REVELATIONS 22:12
Behold I am coming soon bringing my recompense
with me to repay each one for what he has done
I am the Alpha and the Omega the first and last
the beginning and the end.

PURPOSELYDRIVENPOEMS.COM

PURPOSELY DRIVEN POEMS

SHOUT

We can judge
right from wrong if
our discernment is strong
When the day comes
to doubt let the
Ten Commandments out
You could always
get clout to revive
what your about
eliminate your doubt
awaken to God with a shout
let your good spirit
be about
add his living waters
to your drought
all things will work out
SHOUT

PROVERBS 3:5
*Trust in the Lord with all thy heart
lead not into your own understanding
in all thine ways acknowledge him
and he will direct thy path.*

PURPOSELYDRIVENPOEMS.COM

PURPOSELY DRIVEN POEMS

THE GIFT

God gave you a gift
Especially for you
When you realized that what will you do
Would you spread it around
Or would you tuck it away
to save it for someone else
on their rainy day
Now you know it's yours to share
however you choose
or to keep it as a secret never to use
gifts are something to give and receive
so people can feel something in between
it's a double-edged sword
to make you both smile
Maybe for a minute
or a longer while
every time you do
you must believe
anytime you give
you really receive

ROMANS 1:29
For the gifts and calling of God
are without repentance.

PURPOSELYDRIVENPOEMS.COM

ALL YOU GOT

As a fisher of men
you don't need a hook
but it helps if you know
how to spread
the words from his book
sometimes you just read them
sometimes you preach
your fruits of the spirit
are always in reach
his commandments call you
they whisper they knock
there are times in your life
you must
give it all you got

MATTHEW 4:19
*And he said unto them Follow me,
I will make you fishers of men.*

PURPOSELY DRIVEN POEMS

THIS RESIDENCE

One blood one plan to make it work
one God his power
every second of the hour
in his image by his hand
true love for all man
a chosen faith in a perfect time
from our hearts to our minds
everything we can feel
inside to make us real
take another chance
rejoice and let your spirit dance
his words give us spiritual
peace and power
continuing miracles are his true evidence
God rules this residence

ROMANS 13:1
Let every soul be subject unto the higher powers.
For there is no power but of God.
The powers that be are ordained of God.

PURPOSELY DRIVEN POEMS

THE LORDS GRAPES

These are my grapes
growing on my vine
some will grow ripe
to make my wine
but some will drop off
to land on the floor
they won't grow ripe to be
with our lord anymore
if this was a game
how would you score?

JERIMIAH 8:13
I will surely consume them saith the Lord,
There shall be no grapes on the Vine
no figs on the fig tree and the leaf shall fade,
And the things that I have given them
shall pass away from them.

PURPOSELYDRIVENPOEMS.COM

HIS CROWN

He gave us a heart
so we could live with a beat
He blessed us with dreams and hopes
not to live with defeat
He provided our legs
so we can stand tall
He imagined our eyes
so we could see it all
He created a smile
so we never have to frown
and on top of our heads
we are wearing his Crown

JAMES 1:12
*Blessed is the man that endureth temptation
for when he is tried, he shall receive the crown of life
which the lord has promised to those who love him.*

JUST PRAY

The Lord has his poetry
with enough wisdom
to amaze us all
we all share his words
to only want more
we know of his covenant
experienced his rhymes
to receive a power
that is from him
at any given time
you just pray

JEREMIAH 29:12
*Then you will call upon me
and come and pray to me,
and I will hear you.*

FAMILY TREE

We all entered this life
on the day we were born
no flashing lights
no honking horns
no one could stand
but we came to be
at the birth
of our first day born a baby
as we entered the world
of what had to be
we became a leaf
on our family tree

JOHN 3:6
*That which is born of the flesh is flesh,
that which is born of the spirit is spirit.*

OUR PURPOSE

God created a plan
for each one of us
in our beautiful life
called the human purpose
he knew from the beginning
we would find the right purpose
at the right time
it would hold truth
in our hearts and mind
other's too would find
their own in time
it's all for one and one for all
when your human purpose
gives you a call
in our own way
we each feel our truth
it speaks to us each day
it started in our youth.

EPHESIANS 1:11
In whom also we have obtained an inheritance predestined according to the purpose of him who worketh all things after the counsel of his own will.

PURPOSELYDRIVENPOEMS.COM

BEAUTIFUL SMILE

We convey our dreams
we carry our scars
we display our achievements
whatever they are
we explore past life experience
from the memories
hidden deep in our thoughts
the people we knew
but somehow got lost
yes we carry what we can
for the longest human while
but the one thing we
carry the best
is our beautiful smile

PROVERBS 15:30
*A cheerful look brings joy to the heart,
good news makes for good health.*

BLESSINGS

Let us count our blessings
that take us through each day
they emanate our feelings
so our life could have a say
to touch to see to feel
that everything is great
God is so good to us
not his day
shall we ever waste

PSALMS 103:2
Bless the Lord, O my soul; and let us forget not all his benefits.

LISTEN SOME MORE

It is not just money
that makes you rich
but the fruits of the spirit
can do the trick
we all crave a life of luxury
we all want more
but respect your Holy Spirit
it forms your inner core
when Jesus speaks
he speaks to us all
If you don't catch his spirit
you better listen some more

HEBREWS 3:7
Therefore, as the Holy Spirit says
today if you will hear his voice
do not harden your hearts as in the rebellion.

MEANT TO BE

With my moments of thought
and my moments of time
moments of motion
ideas come to mind
today is my day
but how I got here
each cloud rains down the memories
of my past years
so I think back
as far as I can see
today I am still alive
I guess it was meant to be

PSALMS 40:8
I delight to do your will, O my God
Yeah, the law is within my heart.

SALVATION

The ripest fruit
comes from the tree
that Jesus waters so easily
he shared his values
for all to know there in the book
that feeds our soul
the words come easy to understand
you need no dictionary nor foreign hand
to subjugate or translate
or give you directions to heaven's gate
you don't need a GPS
it's not too far
your salvation starts
wherever you are

JOHN 2:17
*The world is passing away
along with its desires but whoever does the will of
God abides forever.*

PURPOSELY DRIVEN POEMS

THE PREACHER MAN

The devil is a sly little fox
he can purloin your faith
to then lock it in a box
when you need it the most
it's just not there
this could make you stamp your feet on the ground
and throw your hands up in the air
all this time Jesus is watching over you
he gave us The Bible,
to help us know what to do
the answers we need are written in the book
it's up to us to read it
not just to give it a little look
it's written in plain English
to help you understand
if you have any other questions
just ask a friendly preacher man

2 TIMOTHY 3:16
*All scripture is God breathed
and is useful for teaching,
rebuking, correcting and training in righteousness.*

PURPOSELYDRIVENPOEMS.COM

KEEP US STRONG

God is here with us each day
he reaches out across the milky way
he dances on stars he lights up the sun
his grace sprinkles down on everyone
he rules the weather that makes our day
his guidance comes to us
in many different ways
in the morning
when we pray along
he builds our faith
to keep us strong

JOB 22:12
Is not God in the height of heaven?
Look also at the distant stars,
How high they are.

EVERY TIME

A seed of faith can grow in you
if you read the word you may find this true
the more you feed the more it grows
your inner spirit will come to know
the seed of faith is all you need
to spark your spirit and believe
so use your patience to seek and find
and God will bless you every time

PSALM 67:6
*The Earth has yielded its produce
O God, our God has blessed us.*

SHAPED FOR SERVING GOD

Shaped for serving God
that is how we came to be
to serve him in this life
then move on to eternity
we are all shaped for serving God
tall, short, round
whatever your shape
a purpose he has found
shaped for serving God
take it slow, fast, or smart
you can do your absolute best
if you ever start
shaped for serving God
in any way you can
as you enjoy his beautiful world
and love your fellow man
shaped for serving God
rewards you every way
your personal inner secret
to share with someone today

CORINTHIANS 12:6
*There are different kinds of working,
but in all of them and everyone
It is the same God at work.*

PURPOSELY DRIVEN POEMS

OUR CHALLENGE…

We cannot allow ourselves to be desensitized by the social inadequacies of negative TV, or the inconsiderate associates of the monster media.

By accepting the desires of the flesh you reduce your Holy Spirit from interceding in accordance with the righteousness of God.

GALATIONS 5:12
The desires of the flesh and desires of the spirit are opposite each other.

So don't let allow your immediate gratification take you astray.

There are 4-D's that you need to be aware of today:

Distraction, dislocation, deceived, destroyed.

AMEN

PURPOSELYDRIVENPOEMS.COM

PURPOSELY DRIVEN POEMS

HIDDEN SO WELL

Millions of Stars
high in the sky
supported in space for Angels to fly
they all shine so bright
only light years away
are they all part of Heaven
will we find out someday
as we stand on the Earth
looking up at evening lights
some so far away
they drift out of sight
we only can wonder
as the question calls why
the Heavens of the Earth
are way up in the Sky
if we ever find out
who can we tell
the mysteries of life
are hidden so well

GENESIS 15:5
*He was taken outside to look up at the Heavens
and was told to count the Stars if you are able
to count them so shall your descendants be.*

PURPOSELY DRIVEN POEMS

WHEN YOU TRY

Build your Faith
make a plan
learn a scripture if you can
absorb the word
passed on to Man
get experience
all just to understand
it is your Faith
you must try
to build it stronger
as your time flies by
when it comes in handy
you'll understand why
Faith grows stronger
when you try

ACTS 15:5
*So the churches were being
strengthened in the Faith,
and were increasing in numbers daily*.

PURPOSELYDRIVENPOEMS.COM

PURPOSELY DRIVEN POEMS

GIFT OF INSIGHT

Your moral compass
can keep you straight
as supplications build our inner faith
he provided you the time and space
to enjoy this life in our eternal race
follow God and his Holy light
your given a moral
night vision compass
to direct your plight
as he designed the exclusive balance
for your moves and might
Gods written words
can thunder in the night
to truly give you
the gift of insight

2ND TIMOTHY 2:10
Consider what I say for the Lord will give you the insight, understanding everything

PURPOSELYDRIVENPOEMS.COM

PURPOSELY DRIVEN POEMS

NO MISTAKES

Faith is a ladder
each step you must climb
God set the directions
you make the time
ever so firmly
each step you are destined to take
as your Spirit keeps rising
God knows no mistakes
the ladder of Faith
as colossal as you need
each step you take
strengthens your belief
we all love God's ladder
with insight we find
we can dance in his mercy
and learn with the patience of time
ever more firmly each step we take
our spirit keeps rising
God makes no mistakes

2 PETER 1:5
*So devote yourselves to lavishly
supplementing your Faith with goodness
and to goodness add understanding.
and to understand to add the strength of self-control.*

PURPOSELYDRIVENPOEMS.COM

PURPOSELY DRIVEN POEMS

YOUR PURPOSE

The call of the day
begins a new start
but the grip of the world
can pull at your heart
tricky wicky world
can even throws darts
just enlighten your senses
so no relationships give blight
or that may start a furious fire
like a little spark might
feeling uncomfortable
can lead you into the dark
so then all the demons
know right where you are
the pretense of the world
says so much to do
but it has to wait when
your purpose calls you

PROVERBS 19:21
Many are the plans in a person's heart, but it is the Lord's purpose that prevails.

PURPOSELYDRIVENPOEMS.COM

PURPOSELY DRIVEN POEMS

AMEN

Amen I say
at the end of the prayer
Amen I say to show God I care
we call this word
to soothe our minds
it sings in the world
since the beginning of time
it holds the promise
that things will be
better after said
for you and me
and so this word
continues and grows
this is the word the whole world
has come to know
AMEN

JAMES 4:2
*Submit yourself therefore to God
Resist the Devil and Evil
will flee from you. Amen.*

PURPOSELYDRIVENPOEMS.COM

TO OBTAIN FAITH

God places in our hands the absolute means whereby Faith can be produced
The responsibility rests with us to seek and find and produce it in our Hearts by our belief and actions

ROMANS 10:8
But what saith? The word is nigh thee, even in thy mouth
and in thine heart: that is the word of Faith, which we preach.

PURPOSELY DRIVEN POEMS

ME AND YOU

We all love Angels
they're like a dream on a star
we all pray to the Heavens
wherever we are
if we all take the time
for one simple action
that would partake someone else
their own Angel satisfaction
then they too
could pass it forward true
to someone new
so the world can be
a better place
for me and you

HEBREWS 1:14
*Angels are ministering spirits
that carry out the bidding of the creator.*

PURPOSELYDRIVENPOEMS.COM

PURPOSELY DRIVEN POEMS

SHINING ON YOU

When things are darkest
you need some light
just ask Jesus his words ring bright
he inspires the hope incisive in your mind
that travels through your bones
in the speed of time
with only Gods beacon of light
can the dark not be
he created the same delights
that can bind you and me
for those that seek they shall find
God is the brightest
Star to ever shine
and when you believe this truth too
you will never want his light
to stop shining on you

EPHESIANS 5:8
*For at one time you were darkness
but now you are light in the lord
walk as children of light.*

PURPOSELYDRIVENPOEMS.COM

PURPOSELY DRIVEN POEMS

STAND TALL

We come to celebrate
we come to rejoice
we come to pray
it is our choice
here we are no rhythm shall we lose
a greater power we chose to choose
he who catches us if we should fall
with open ears we hear God's call
exceptional is his Grace
with so much more
when you are a Christian
you will stand tall

1 CORINTHIANS 16:13
*Listen, stay alert, stand tall
in the Faith, be courageous and be strong.*

PURPOSELYDRIVENPOEMS.COM

EVERYTHING

Pictures in your mind
will never go away
they are exchanged
in your memory
for another living day
never shall we forget
to pray to laugh and sing
to ingratiate with all the beauty
the world can bring
as we share our love
with everything

PROVERBS 16:3
*Commit thy works unto the Lord
and thy thoughts shall be established.*

PURPOSELY DRIVEN POEMS

WORDS

All words are alive
in sight and sound
the words that live in
his scriptures
echo the world around
as we must hear and stay alert
to acknowledge what they say
teaching our Lord's values
from his choice lessons
he knows won't go away
words have their meaning
yet to convey
the words that you hear
can do more than they say
they can rearrange your thoughts
to change your whole day
they can emancipate
your old memories
that seem to never go away

MATHEW 12:37
*For by the words thou shalt be justified
or by the words thy shall be condemned*.

PURPOSELYDRIVENPOEMS.COM

LORD GODS POEM

Every prayer is like a poem
the blessings to come
won't leave you alone
they create a spiritual blanket
to rest each soul
while you feed your Faith
down to the bone
never without
or ever alone
all prayers create an
emanating tone
as his grace does expel
from the Lord Gods poem
words from our Lord
never leave you alone
they are here to love
and protect your home

HEBREWS 4:10
*The word of God is quick and powerful,
sharper than any two edged sword.*

FAITH IS A SONG

Faith is a word
that belongs in a song
so all believers
can sing along
when you listen real close
you can hear it beat
faith has a winning tune
that plays no defeat
what I have seen helps me to know
as I play the song
my perseverance only grows
providing the hope
to make myself go
alluring to the road that i need so
Faith is the song
we all need to know

JAMES 1:3
*Because you know
that the testing of your faith
produces perseverance*.

SO GOOD

I see the Moon
it projects its own light
above me each day
a full circle or slice
miracles can happen
everywhere I look
they continue each day
to make me feel good

JOHN 16:33
*These things I have spoken unto you
that in me ye might have peace
In the world you shall have tribulation
but be of good cheer
I have overcome the world.*

PURPOSELY DRIVEN POEMS

YOU ARE NEVER ALONE

Angel here Angel there
zipping around everywhere
across the ground
through the air
angels of flight are everywhere
they christian in the day
they ignite the night
to bless our Faith
all Angels delight
spreading God's graces
we need so
to receive the strength
to tell the devil no
they fly in groups they fly alone
the guardian Angels are God's drones
when you believe in God
then you are never alone

PSALM 91:11
For he shall give his Angels charge over thee,
to keep thee, in all thy ways.
They shall bear thee up in their hands,
lest thou dash thy foot against a stone.

PURPOSELYDRIVENPOEMS.COM

PURPOSELY DRIVEN POEMS

BEFORE

A smile comes along easy
to move throughout your day
but then this magnificent surprise
just somehow slips away
so now you must think
beautiful thoughts
of Heaven some more
to get back the smile
you once had before

PSALM 37:4
*Take delight in the lord, and he will
give you the desires of your heart.*

PURPOSELY DRIVEN POEMS

BRIGHTEN YOUR DAY

God's Earth is a playground
for all spirits to play
they dance and sing songs
about life and the way
God knows how to add true color
to a life that is gray
and turn on
all your spiritual blessings
to brighten your day

ROMANS 8:31
*What, then, shall we say in response
to these things?
If God is for us,
who can be against us?*

PURPOSELYDRIVENPOEMS.COM

PURPOSELY DRIVEN POEMS

THE TONGUE

Your tongue has the power
all its own
to be the sharpest sword
you will ever own
it can cut to the truth
or chop up a lie
it can hit all the high notes
like a baby's cry
the tongue has more power
than you have ever known
it gives you the ability to speak on your own
so every blessed day you prosper and grow
with knowledge to learn wisdom to show
it allows yourself to purposely thrive
in Faith, Hope and Love
all the days you're alive

1 PETER 3:10
*For he that loves life, and sees good days,
let him refrain his tongue from evil and his lips speak
no guile.*

PURPOSELYDRIVENPOEMS.COM

PURPOSELY DRIVEN POEMS

GOOD OLD TIME

Positive affirmations
come from your mouth
when you fly like a spirit
you are never without
God sent a melody
to bring harmony
to our hearts and mind
as we ingratiate into this life
that delivers so fine
as we keep enjoying
a good old time
because everybody
wants a good old time

PSALM 119:105
*Thy word is a lamp unto my feet
and a light unto my path.*

PURPOSELYDRIVENPOEMS.COM

PURPOSELY DRIVEN POEMS

CHRISTMAS DAY

He was born under the star light
of an ebony sky
the son of our Father
whom we hold most high
he arrived in the world
to spread the truth and the way
for people of the world with faith
to follow today
he was named Jesus saviour and king
three wise men ventured out
with presents to bring
Holy he radiated they all found him to be
the true blessed baby
for our world's history
when all of the miracles
we ever could dream
happen on earth
for believers to see
Holy so Holy for all followers to say
Jesus the saviour
Born Christmas day

LUKE 2:11
*Today in the town of Bethlehem
a saviour has been born to you.
He is the messiah, the Lord.*

PURPOSELYDRIVENPOEMS.COM

PURPOSELY DRIVEN POEMS

START

Here comes a little air
so we could breathe
without a care
allow us to live
for times to be
to give us freedom
so easily
do we take all this air for granted?
because it never ever parts
we'll acknowledge this
without a breath of
God's fresh air
our day would never ever start

JOB 33:4
*The spirit of God has made me
and the breath of the Almighty gives me life.*

PURPOSELYDRIVENPOEMS.COM

PURPOSELY DRIVEN POEMS

TREE OF FAITH

The tree of faith
starts with the seed
that can grow as fast
as you believe
branches reach out
from you and I to the heavens
hopes way up in the sky
roots get nourishment
from the earth
to grow up strong with
wonder and work
our faith grows strong
just like a tree
the way
God planned it to be

PSALM 52:8
*But I am like a green Olive tree
in the house of the Lord
I trust in the mercy of God
forever and ever.*

PURPOSELYDRIVENPOEMS.COM

PURPOSELY DRIVEN POEMS

GOD'S DRONES

Angel here Angel there
zipping around everywhere
they fly each day
they sail the night
they bless us all
it's their delight
to sprinkle God's grace
we need it so
the come in groups
or they come alone
the guardian angels
make it known
The Guardian Angels
are God's drones

PSALM 91:11
*For he shall give his angels charge
over thee to keep thee in all thy ways.*

PURPOSELYDRIVENPOEMS.COM

PURPOSELY DRIVEN POEMS

THE SONG OF LIFE

The song of life
starts with the poem
the dancing words
won't leave you alone
they create a rhythm
all their own
to warm your blood
and move your bones
the song of life
words from a poem
when the melody comes
it won't leave you alone
each song of life
implores the tone
so the touching words
never leave you alone

EPHESIANS 2:10
*We have become his poetry
a re-created people that will fulfill
the destiny God planned in advance
for us and the good works
we would do to fulfill it.*

PURPOSELYDRIVENPOEMS.COM

PURPOSELY DRIVEN POEMS

EACH STEP

Each step that you take
helps you to achieve
those times in your life
when you've come to receive
the blessings from Angels
pure grace from the Lord
and love from Jesus our Savior
whom we've come to adore

PROVERBS 3:6
*With each step you take
think about what the Lord wants
and he will help lead you go the right way.*

PURPOSELYDRIVENPOEMS.COM

PURPOSELY DRIVEN POEMS

OUR LORD

We all have ideas
they come when they do
they open closed doors
so we could get through
it's natural and proactive
need I say more
the keys to the Kingdom
are held in the book
of our Lord

LUKE 12:32
Fear not, little flock, for it is your father's great pleasure to give you the kingdom.

PURPOSELYDRIVENPOEMS.COM

PURPOSELY DRIVEN POEMS

A SPIRIT

We each have a spirit
it simmers inside
individually unique
with the perfect design
it really radiates from us
so others can surely see
the aura of our spirit so easily
spirit like the heart
lives inside
it travels all around
wherever we might fly
just feed your spirit up
so it will never let you down
let your fruits of the spirit
reflect a perfect crown

PSALM 51:10
Create in me a clean heart
O God and renew
A right spirit in me.

PURPOSELYDRIVENPOEMS.COM

PURPOSELY DRIVEN POEMS

ONE DAY

The world is emotion
with pleasure and pain
we feel all the emotions
and they're never the same
they come when they want
whether were ready or not
some emotions are so amazing
they never forgot
emotions of laughter
or crying when you may
so many emotions
in your life can happen
in one day

MATTHEW 11:28
*Come to me all you who are weary
and burdened
And I will give you rest.*

PURPOSELYDRIVENPOEMS.COM

PURPOSELY DRIVEN POEMS

EVERYBODY

Thank you Jesus
you did me right
you allow my feet
to walk under your light
what was dark is now so bright
and I follow your words
to give my spirit flight
these times in the scriptures
have been talking to me
they help me now
to be able to see
the truth in the world
how to be free
that simple spirit
speaks
to everybody

JUDE 1:21
Keep yourself in the love of God
looking for the mercy of our lord
Jesus Christ unto eternal life.

PURPOSELY DRIVEN POEMS

EVERY HOUR

Hope is a word
so small but so fine
hope is a word to inspire your mind
hope is a word for believers to know
cause it follows their Faith
wherever they go
hope has an energy
it gives your life a power
to keep your Faith winning
every day every hour

ROMANS 8:24
For we are saved by hope,
But hope that is seen is not hope.
For what a man seethe why does he yet hope for
But if we hope for what we see not
Then do we with patience wait for it.

PURPOSELYDRIVENPOEMS.COM

CAN'T BE DENIED

Thank you, Jesus, for this bed
as I tuck my pillow under my head
laying here looking up at the sky
visions of angels as spirits fly
the thoughts in my mind
just float on by
I stand my ground
the Lord knows why
for the messages I hear
Can't be denied

JOHN 10:27
*My sheep hear my voice, and I know them
they listen, to follow me.*

CULTIVATE YOUR DREAMS

Hope is a vessel alive in the world
exploring the oceans for oysters and pearls
hope is an emotion a small word to believe
that you could be anything you want to achieve
hope is the progression you may gently bestow
to uplift your friends and help them all grow
hope is the flavor we all need to taste
so desires of our heart
won't go to waste
hope gives you the promise
for the grass to go green
a positive motivational thought
to cultivate your dreams

PSALM 32:8
I will instruct you and teach you in the way thou shall go. I will guide thee with thine eye.

NEVER FORGOT

As a Fisher of men
you don't need a hook
but it helps if you know
how to spread
the words
from his book
sometimes you read
sometimes you preach
your fruits of the spirit
are always in reach
his commandments call you
they whisper they knock
there are times in your life
that are never forgot

MATTHEW 4:19
*And he said unto them follow me,
I will make you fishers of men.*

PURPOSELY DRIVEN POEMS

JESUS TELLS US SO

The Lord
is with me
and my spirit
and so
the story grows
He led his life He leads my life
everybody knows
when you stand as a Christian
you must be on your toes
our path is very narrow
Jesus tells us so

LUKE 6:46
*Why do you call me Lord
and not follow what I say?*

PURPOSELYDRIVENPOEMS.COM

PURPOSELY DRIVEN POEMS

EVER SO STRONG

When you take time to pray
Jesus could surely bless your day
he is only there to carry your burden
whether you believe it or not
he's the one
that was hurting
he took our punishment
ever so strong
and now we are free
to sing his song
so his story just
carries along
ever, ever, ever so strong

PROVERBS 3:5
Trust in the Lord with all thy heart and lean not on your own understanding.

PURPOSELY DRIVEN POEMS

BE

Be fruitful multiply
don't be shy
reach out in life
so no one can deny
speak out your peace
lead on with no doubt
hold out your helping hand
to others lost in the crowd
take dominion in your life
keep open your eyes
be thankful where you stand
Be fruitful and multiply

GENESIS 1:28
*God blessed them and said
Be fruitful and multiply
And replenish the Earth.*

PURPOSELYDRIVENPOEMS.COM

PURPOSELY DRIVEN POEMS

STILL

God made the world
for all of us to enjoy
each and every girl
every little boy
we grew up into adults
to live a life so full
while emotions move us every day
with so many to fulfill
so this busy
world we're in
never leaves us still

MATTHEW 11:28
*Come to me all ye
that labor and are heavily laden
and I will give you rest.*

PURPOSELYDRIVENPOEMS.COM

PURPOSELY DRIVEN POEMS

OURS TO HOLD

Holy Holy Easter day
the air is quiet when people pray
all prayers to him
came from us
on his birth they named him
baby Jesus
the emancipation of his life had come
the Lord's word said
thy will be done
his father's spirit
shined the light
for people in the world to see so bright
one dark spring day, without a frost
they took his body off the cross
as we knelt in sacred union
to receive his first Holy Communion
on this day as it all unfolds
his memory becoming ours to hold

JOHN 3:16
For God so loved the world
that he gave his only begotten son
that whosoever believeth in Him
will not perish but shall have eternal life.

PURPOSELYDRIVENPOEMS.COM

ECHO TODAY

The Lord is alive
for those that may pray
his spirit brings hope
to brighten your day
his scriptures add color
to the words that we read
our faith can acknowledge
what we've all come to believe
the Lord's not a mystery
and he has no true rival
his life story can be read anytime
in the Bible
for those who inquire
can always find out
his miracles all happened
no Christian could doubt
for all that is sacred
and blessed by his way
the words spread by Jesus
still echo today

MARK 16:15
*And he said unto them, go into the world
and preach the gospel to every creature.*

PURPOSELY DRIVEN POEMS

THE MESSAGE

There is always a message
we can receive
which speaks to us everyday
with thoughts to believe
we experience it at times
we need it the most
it comes with the strength
from our inner Holy Ghost
this can be divine
just know it is true
God sends his message of love
to me and to you

JOHN 3:16
*God so loves the world
he sent his only begotten son
who shall believe in him shall
never perish but have everlasting life.*

PURPOSELYDRIVENPOEMS.COM

PURPOSELY DRIVEN POEMS

I AM CONTENT

The words in the song
say we have to get along
in a principle part of the powerful play
which allows the work
that we do everyday
it sure keeps us alive
with our spirit of insight
God guides us when we listen
and he blesses our life
and gives us the flavors
that keep tasting so right
as we enjoy each magnificent moonlight
just to bring us more delight
now looking back I wonder
how my time just came and went
it sure makes me smile though
because now i am content

1 TIMOTHY 6:6
But godliness with contentment is great gain.

TO FLOW

The path of your love
the path of your life
the path of the moment
we hope it's just right
as we live each day
running out of hours
we speak with
our weakness
or the spirit of power
you know this
so when
you get up to leave
because
it's time to go
you smile
nod your head
and tiptoe to flow

JOHN 1:28
*He that believeth in me
like the Scripture hath says,
out of his belly shall flow rivers of water.*

PURPOSELYDRIVENPOEMS.COM

PURPOSELY DRIVEN POEMS

DISGUISE

Some people you meet
you forget not because they are part
of your future
that can't be forgot
it's tricky it's simple it's a proactive design
moving you forward in your actions and time
a super surprise will be waiting
at the end of the trail
if you shall reach it
it's to your avail
so stay focused
keep your eye on the prize
and don't be fooled
by the generic disguise

EPHESIANS 1:11
*Put on the whole armour of God,
that you may be able to stand
against the wiles of the devil.*

PURPOSELYDRIVENPOEMS.COM

ON FIRE

We all have a purpose
and we all have a style
we walk with our sway
and we all laugh and we smile
as we know we have the needs
hopes and desires
as we all have inspiration
that sets
our imagination on fire

1st Corinthians 3:13
*The work will be shown for what it is
because the day will bring it to light.
It will be revealed with fire, and the fire
will test the quality of each person's work.*

VICTORY

I wake up each morning
to a new day's sun
I arrange my moments
one by one
I stay positive and proactive
I keep moving along
this is my day
my winning is strong
My victory is coming
I am prepared for much more
to live life to the fullest
and keep on winning for all

ROMANS 12:21
*Be not overcome of evil,
but overcome evil with good.*

PURPOSELY DRIVEN POEMS

ANOTHER BEAUTIFUL DAY

We are born in the flesh
we read by the light
we follow the moves
we think that are right
we accept what we can
applaud all we do
we are the people of the world
can you feel me and share my view?
Words come across
to interest or amuse
or criticize and condemn
depends how you use
we look forward to
persuade and convince
all people that still are straddling the fence
with all of God's goodness coming our way
let's enjoy another beautiful day

MATTHEW 6:24
No man can serve two masters
For either he will hate one, and love the other
Or be loyal to one, and despise the other
Christian straddling the fence are trying
to serve two masters.

PURPOSELYDRIVENPOEMS.COM

PURPOSELY DRIVEN POEMS

THE MIGHT

Refuse to be a victim
stand for your rights
refuse to be a victim
don't lose the fight
refuse to be a victim
you have a power in your life
his breath gave you your spirit
God gives you
the might
victory starts in your thinking
turn on your light

JAMES 5:13
Is any among you afflicted?
Let them pray
Is any merry? Let them sing.

PURPOSELYDRIVENPOEMS.COM

PURPOSELY DRIVEN POEMS

SHINE

Our faith in the Lord comes from within
it breeds us exuberance with confidence
as we look up with our chin
we know of the light
and the road that we walk
one helps us to see
one helps us to talk
he launches the colors
for his spirits to show
he brings us to grass
that God only grows
positive with patience
as we embellish our times
because Christ Jesus is with us
to make us all shine

NUMBERS 6:24
The Lord bless thee, and keep thee
The Lord make his face shine upon thee
and be gracious under thee.

PURPOSELYDRIVENPOEMS.COM

HOPE TODAY

Hope is a shadow
it follows you around
it has his own opinion
but doesn't make a sound
it relies upon your power
as it depends
upon your say
the hope you carry
inside of you
is the hope
you need today

ROMANS 15:13
Now the God of hope
fills you with all the peace in believing
that you may abound in hope
through the Holy Ghost.

A GOOD TIME

Responsibility is part of your life
what you do in the dark
will always come to light
you can fool your mother
you can lie to your friend
But God sees through you
all the way to the end
so with this thought
now stuck in your mind
say a prayer of thanks
and go have a good time

EPHESIANS 3:20
*Now unto him that is able to do.
Exceeding abundantly
above all that we ask or think.
According to the power that worketh within us.*

PURPOSELY DRIVEN POEMS

ALLOW IT TO BE

Motion to motion
minute by minute
we cherish God's word
and what goes with it
it allows us to grow it allows us to smile
allows us to share
and live with a style
all I can say this I know
God's word gets louder as it continues to grow
it taught us then
teaches us now
with the wonders of the world
that makes us go wow
his words explain the why
of what will be
as each day becomes as good
as you allow it to be

MICAH 6:8
*He has shown you O mortal what is good
and what does the Lord require of you.*

PURPOSELYDRIVENPOEMS.COM

PURPOSELY DRIVEN POEMS

ALL IT CAN BE

Live for the moment
each moment is life
for a purpose you live
to create what you like
it might be the best
it might be the worst
but it brings you the truth
to quench all your thirst
our instinct of insight
when your dreams can be seen
in the life that you live
passes so easy
if you just open your eyes
and act purposely
your future in life
passes by like a breeze

EPHESIANS 4:32
*And be kind to one another
tenderhearted forgiving one another
even God for Christ's sake forgive you.*

PURPOSELYDRIVENPOEMS.COM

PURPOSELY DRIVEN POEMS

GRATITUDE

Express your gratitude
to be happy and free
give it out to the world
for all to see
brothers and sisters
young and old men
the gratitude you start
will never just end
the gratitude attitude
is somewhere to be
when you walk in the darkness
the light you won't see
when you walk in the darkness
a smile just can't be

COLOSSIANS 3:15
*And let the peace of God rule in your heart
to which, also ye are called
in one body and be ye thankful.*

PURPOSELY DRIVEN POEMS

MY DESTINY

I stand right here
to openly declare
I am a magnet to blessings
with the scriptures I share
I turn on my radar so my spirit can find
Harmony and peace
as Jesus shares my time
troubles follow sinners
blessings follow believers
the way you choose
is the way you receive it
and every day I am more grateful
for whatever just might be
because God
has His hand on my destiny

PSALMS 31:15
My life, my every moment, my destiny it's all in your hands. So I know you can deliver me from those who persecute me relentlessly.

PURPOSELYDRIVENPOEMS.COM

PURPOSELY DRIVEN POEMS

PURPOSELY DRIVEN

A purpose that's driven
is all that you need
to put forth the energy
to help you achieve
the reason for action
harbouring high hope
making mega moves
can accomplish the most
speaking a language
that genius demands
with evolving new revelations
that delightfully dictate your plan
this may all implement
a desire you know
to keep you purposely driven
with all systems go

2ND CORINTHIANS 9:7
*Every man accordingly as he purposeth in his heart
so let him give, not grudgingly, or of necessity
for God loves a cheerful giver.*

PURPOSELYDRIVENPOEMS.COM

PURPOSELY DRIVEN POEMS

When you find your favourite poem from any book, you can order it in Canvas to hang on your wall and inspire your home. To get 25% off, login to Purposelydrivenpoems.com and enter code PDP2022.

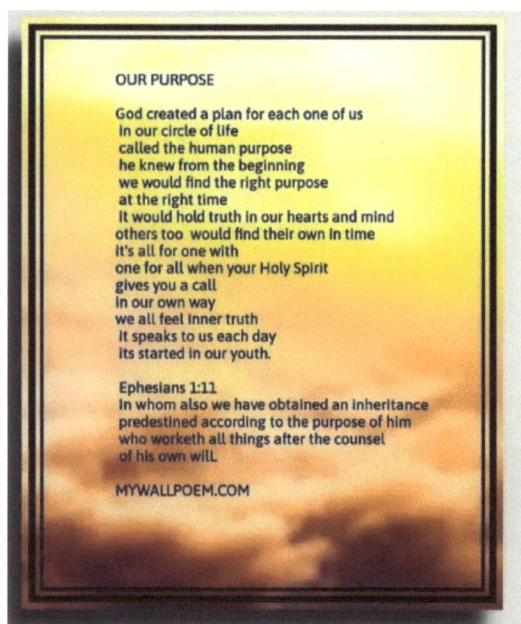

PURPOSELYDRIVENPOEMS.COM

PURPOSELY DRIVEN POEMS

*If you enjoyed **Purposely Driven Poems**, I would really appreciate a short review, your help in spreading the word is highly valued and reviews make it much easier for readers to find the book.*

Review Link:

https://www.amazon.com/review/create-review/?ie=UTF8&channel=glance-detail&asin=B0B324N77R

I welcome questions or comments.

Please Email:

Bill Rockefeller

purposelydrivenpoems@gmail.com

And

Visit my Website:

PURPOSELYDRIVENPOEMS.COM

PURPOSELY DRIVEN POEMS

To get your **FREE** copy of Bill Rockefeller's *The Ten Commandments In Poetry*, click on the link below:

Fill out the form with your name and email address, and in the 'Message' section indicate:

- Title of book: **The Ten Commandments In Poetry**
- Whether you want a **PDF** or **EPUB** file.

Free Book Link:
https://battlepress.media/?page_id=13

Your book will be emailed to you. ENJOY!

*If you enjoyed **Purposely Driven Poems**, I would really appreciate a short review, your help in spreading the word is highly valued and reviews make it much easier for readers to find the book.*

Review Link:
https://www.amazon.com/review/create-review/?ie=UTF8&channel=glance-detail&asin=B0B324N77R

PURPOSELYDRIVENPOEMS.COM